The Conflict Resolution Library™

Dealing with Arguments

• Lisa K. Adams •

The Rosen Publishing Group's
PowerKids Press™
New York

Published in 1997 by The Rosen Publishing Group, Inc.
29 East 21st Street, New York, NY 10010

First Edition

Book Design: Erin McKenna

Photo Credits: Cover © Steven Ferry/P&F Communications; pp. 4, 16, 20 by Seth Dinnerman; pp. 7, 8, 12, 15 © Steven Ferry/P&F Communications; p. 11 by Guillermina DeFerrari; p. 19 © Maria Moreno.

Adams, Lisa K.
    Dealing with arguments / by Lisa K. Adams.
        p.   cm. — (The conflict resolution library)
    Includes index.
    Summary: Discusses what arguments are, how they begin, and ways to solve disagreements without fighting.
    ISBN 0-8239-5073-5
    1. Interpersonal conflict in children—Juvenile literature. 2. Problem solving in children—Juvenile literature. [1. Conflict (Psychology) 2. Quarreling. 3. Interpersonal relations.] I. Title. II. Series.
    BF723.I645A33 1997
    303.6'9—dc21   97-4145
                                                                              CIP
                                                                               AC

Manufactured in the United States of America

Contents

What Is an Argument?

Everyone is **unique** (yoo-NEEK). We are all special and have our own ways of seeing and doing things. That means we will not agree with everybody all the time. It's okay to disagree with someone. But when two people who disagree get angry, an **argument** (AR-gyoo-ment) can start.

Everybody argues sometimes. Arguing is natural. Some arguments can even be helpful. But when some people argue, they often stop listening to each other. These kinds of arguments can be harmful.

◀ Having different ideas is part of being a unique and special person.

How Do Arguments Start?

Arguments can start when one person doesn't like what another person has said or done. People argue about all sorts of things. At school, kids may argue about whose turn it is to use the swing. Or a person may argue to try to change the way another person thinks about something.

But arguing doesn't usually change the way another person thinks. Most arguments leave people feeling even angrier than before.

Arguments can start when people disagree and stop listening to each other. ▶

Talking Calmly

When you were younger, you may have raised your voice or yelled to show other people that you were angry or that you disagreed with them. Now that you are older, you know that raising your voice may start an argument. You can learn to show your anger in better ways.

The best way to let someone know that you're angry or that you disagree is to tell her calmly. Then give her a chance to tell you how she feels. Instead of having an argument, you can have a **discussion** (dis-KUSH-en).

If you have a disagreement with someone else, talking it out is the best way to try to solve the problem.

Listening

One of the most important parts of a discussion is listening. If two people who are having a discussion don't listen to each other, the problem won't get solved.

Listen carefully to what the other person has to say. Let her finish talking before you say what you want to say. Maybe she had a good reason for doing what she did. If you don't listen, you'll never find out her side of the story.

Good friends listen to each other when something is wrong or when they disagree. ▶

Talking

The way you talk during a discussion is just as important as the way you listen. Think about how you feel before you start talking. Try not to get angry. Instead of yelling, talk in a calm voice.

Also, stay on the subject. If you are arguing with your brother about whose turn it is to play with the basketball, don't start calling him names or bring up something else that may be bothering you. **Insults** (IN-sults) don't solve problems.

Discussing different ideas with your
◀ friends helps to avoid arguments.

Two Brothers

Jay's favorite book was missing. When Jay saw Donny reading it, he got mad. But Jay calmly asked Donny why he took the book without asking him first.

Instead of yelling at each other, Jay and Donny discussed the problem. Neither one raised his voice. Donny didn't even know that Jay was looking for the book. Jay **apologized** (uh-POL-uh-jyzd) for thinking Donny had stolen it. Donny asked if he could borrow the book. Jay said yes.

Fighting with each other will only make a problem worse. ▶

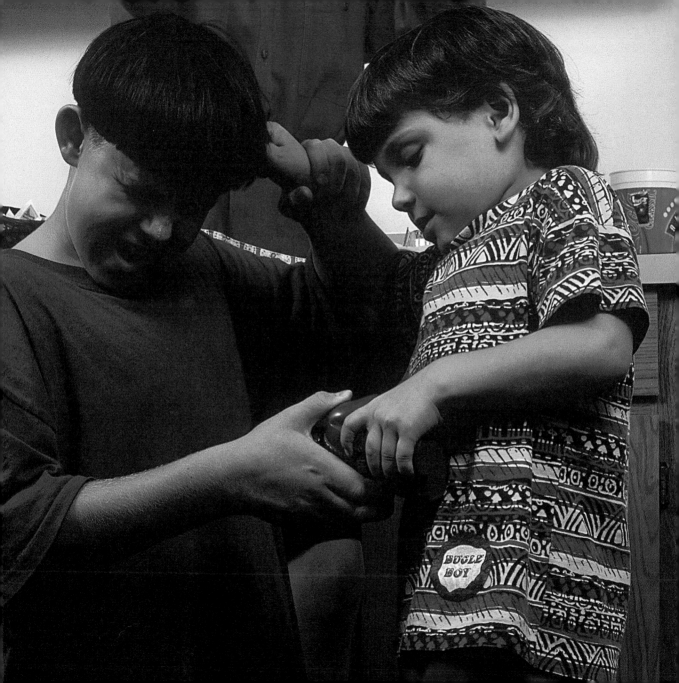

Compromise

Sometimes discussions turn into arguments. This is when the two people need to **compromise** (KOM-pruh-myz) to solve a problem.

When people compromise, each side gives in a little, so both people get some of what they want. This is the best way to make sure an argument or a discussion ends fairly.

Learning to compromise will help you get along much better with others. No one likes a person who insists on having his way all the time or insists that he is always right.

◄ You can easily come to an agreement if you compromise.

Winning and Losing

Often when people argue, they let their **pride** (PRYD) get in the way. They don't want to stop arguing because they don't want to "lose" the argument. But an argument is not a game. There are no winners or losers. It's a bad idea to continue arguing just because you're too proud to say that you might be wrong.

If the argument helps both people understand each other, then both sides have won.

Admitting that you're wrong can be hard to do, but it could ▶
end a hurtful argument between you and a good friend.

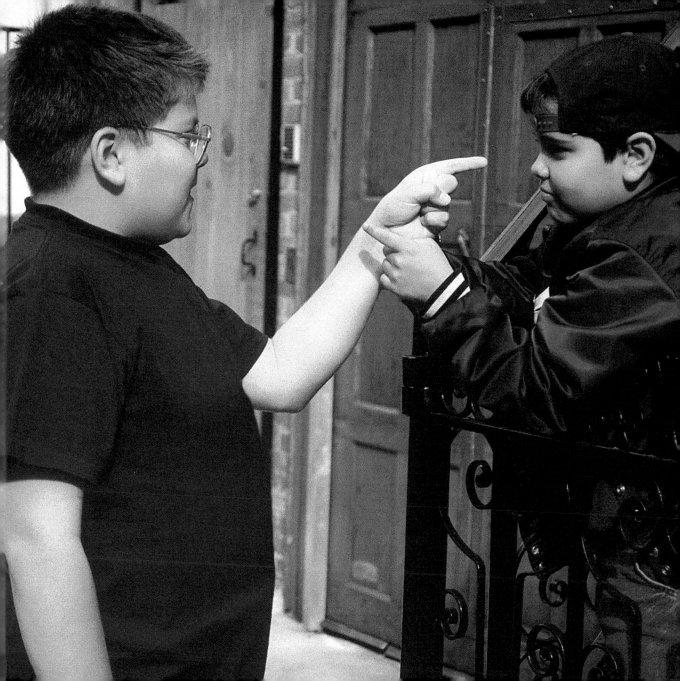

Jennifer and Danica

Jennifer and Danica were working on a worksheet at school. Jennifer told Danica that her answer was stupid. Danica thought her answer was just fine. But she decided not to argue about it because it didn't really matter to her what Jennifer thought.

Both girls went back to their own work. Danica avoided an argument by **ignoring** (ig-NOR-ing) Jennifer. Jennifer learned that starting an argument was a waste of time.

◀ Sometimes people will try to get you to argue with them. If you don't feel like arguing, then just walk away.

Avoiding an Argument

Many arguments can be avoided. If we got into an argument every time we were a little upset about something, we'd be arguing all the time! You have to decide if it's worth your time and energy to argue about something.

If you know that someone is starting an argument with you just to get you mad, don't let him do it. Arguing usually doesn't help anybody. Now you know how to deal with arguments the right way.

Glossary

apologize (uh-POL-uh-jyz) To say you are sorry.

argument (AR-gyoo-ment) When people who don't agree about something get angry at each other.

compromise (KOM-pruh-myz) When two people give up part of what they want to come to an agreement.

discussion (dis-KUSH-en) Talking calmly and listening to someone.

ignore (ig-NOR) To not pay attention to something.

insult (IN-sult) To say something mean to someone.

pride (PRYD) Self-respect that can sometimes get in the way of being fair and reasonable.

unique (yoo-NEEK) Something or someone that is one of a kind.

Index